The Life and Legacy of Stephen Marcos Gonzales: A Journey Through Albuquerque

Stephen G.

Published by Stephen G., 2024.

THIS BOOK IS DEDICATED TO THE
Stephen G. family,
(Author) Stephen G.

Table of Contents

The Life and Legacy of Stephen Marcos Gonzales: A Journey Through Albuquerque

Chapter 1: Early Life and Background
Birth and Family Origins

Stephen Marcos Gonzales was born on August 28, 1985, in the vibrant city of Albuquerque, New Mexico. This culturally rich city, known for its diverse heritage and historical significance, provided a unique backdrop for Gonzales' formative years. Growing up in this environment, he was influenced by the blend of Native American, Hispanic, and Anglo cultures that characterize the region. These early experiences not only shaped his identity but also instilled in him a deep appreciation for the traditions and stories that define Albuquerque.

Gonzales comes from a family with deep roots in New Mexico, which has contributed significantly to his sense of community and belonging. His parents, both active members of their respective communities, emphasized the importance of education, hard work, and civic responsibility. His father, a small business owner, and his mother, a dedicated educator, served as role models for Gonzales, demonstrating the value of service and commitment to one's community. This familial support laid the groundwork for his ambitions and aspirations, encouraging him to pursue his passions while staying connected to his heritage.

The Gonzales family history is rich with narratives that highlight resilience and determination. Stephen's grandparents were integral figures in their neighborhoods, known for their contributions to local initiatives and events. Their legacy of community involvement inspired Stephen to engage in similar efforts as he grew older. Understanding the sacrifices and achievements of his ancestors has motivated him to honor their memory through his own philanthropic endeavors, reinforcing the idea that one's roots can profoundly influence their path in life.

Stephen's upbringing in Albuquerque was also marked by the influence of local traditions and cultural practices. Family gatherings often included storytelling sessions, where elders shared tales that highlighted the importance of cultural identity. These gatherings not only strengthened familial bonds but also instilled in him a sense of pride in his heritage. This cultural grounding became a cornerstone of his identity, influencing his future contributions to the arts and community initiatives in Albuquerque, where he sought to celebrate and promote local culture.

As he grew into adulthood, Stephen Marcos Gonzales emerged as a prominent figure in Albuquerque, known for his contributions across various sectors. His commitment to education and the arts, paired with a passion for community service, propelled him into a career that reflects his values and interests. Through his professional journey, he has remained deeply connected to his family origins, using his platform to uplift and inspire others. His life story serves as a testament to the impact of family heritage and community ties in shaping an individual's journey, and it continues to resonate with many in Albuquerque and beyond.

Childhood in Albuquerque

Childhood in Albuquerque played a significant role in shaping Stephen Marcos Gonzales into the individual he would become. Born on August 28, 1985, in this vibrant city, Stephen's early years were steeped in the rich cultural tapestry of New Mexico. Growing up in a community where diverse traditions coalesced, he was exposed to a variety of languages, cuisines, and customs that enriched his formative experiences. This multicultural environment not only fostered his appreciation for diversity but also instilled in him a deep sense of belonging and identity.

Stephen's family history and heritage were integral to his childhood. He was raised in a household that emphasized the importance of family and community ties. His parents, who hailed from a mix of backgrounds, encouraged him to explore his roots while also respecting and learning from others. The stories shared around the dinner table often featured tales of resilience and hard work, which inspired Stephen to adopt similar values in his own life. These early influences laid the groundwork for his future contributions to Albuquerque, as he learned the value of giving back to the community that nurtured him.

Education was another cornerstone of Stephen's upbringing. Attending local schools in Albuquerque, he excelled academically while also participating in extracurricular activities that sparked his interests. His passion for the arts was evident from an early age, as he engaged in various creative pursuits, from painting to theater. This foundation not only honed his talents but also connected him with mentors who would later influence his career path. Stephen's educational journey was marked by a commitment to lifelong learning, which would become a hallmark of his professional endeavors.

As a child, Stephen was deeply influenced by the local culture and arts that Albuquerque had to offer. The city's rich history, vibrant festivals, and artistic community provided a backdrop for his creative expression. Whether attending local art fairs or participating in community events, Stephen was inspired by the talent and passion of those around him. This exposure instilled in him a desire to contribute to the arts, leading him to become a prominent advocate for local artists and cultural initiatives in his adult life. His childhood experiences in Albuquerque shaped his understanding of the significant role art plays in community cohesion and individual expression.

The impact of Stephen's childhood in Albuquerque can be seen in his philanthropic efforts and initiatives throughout his life. Understanding the importance of community support, he has dedicated himself to various causes that uplift underrepresented groups and promote education in the arts. His connections to his childhood experiences motivate him to create opportunities for the next generation, ensuring that the vibrant culture of Albuquerque continues to thrive. As he reflects on his upbringing, Stephen recognizes that his roots in this remarkable city have been a driving force behind his commitment to making a difference in the lives of others.

Influences and Role Models

Stephen Marcos Gonzales drew inspiration from a rich tapestry of influences and role models throughout his life, shaping him into the prominent figure he became in Albuquerque. Born in 1985, he was raised in a culturally vibrant environment where the legacies of local leaders and artists resonated deeply. His parents instilled in him the values of community service and cultural appreciation, which would later guide his philanthropic endeavors and contributions to the arts. From a young age, he was exposed to the passion of local activists and artists, which ignited his desire to make a meaningful impact in his own community.

As a young adult, Gonzales found role models in various figures, including educators and community organizers who championed social justice and cultural preservation. These individuals not only inspired him to pursue an education but also to engage actively in initiatives that uplifted marginalized voices in Albuquerque. His educational journey, marked by a commitment to learning, led him to seek knowledge that would equip him to address the social issues he witnessed in his community. The encouragement he received from mentors solidified his belief in the transformative power of education, which he later sought to promote through his philanthropic efforts.

In addition to social justice advocates, Gonzales was influenced by local artists who celebrated the unique heritage of Albuquerque. He admired the works of painters, musicians, and writers who captured the essence of the city's diverse culture. This appreciation for the arts influenced his own creative pursuits and fostered a desire to support local talent. Gonzales became a vocal advocate for the arts, recognizing their role in shaping community identity and promoting healing. His involvement in various cultural initiatives underscored his belief that art not only enriches lives but also serves as a powerful tool for social change.

Gonzales' role models extended to those in the business sector who demonstrated integrity and innovation. He observed how successful entrepreneurs conducted their affairs with a sense of responsibility toward their communities. Inspired by their example, he sought to incorporate similar values into his own career. This led him to pursue opportunities that not only advanced his professional aspirations but also contributed to the economic development of Albuquerque. His ability to blend personal success with community benefit became a hallmark of his career, allowing him to serve as a role model for aspiring business leaders in the area.

Ultimately, the influences and role models in Stephen Marcos Gonzales' life shaped his journey in profound ways. From his family's enduring values to the lessons learned from community leaders and artists, each influence contributed to his holistic approach to life and service. Gonzales' legacy is a testament to the power of mentorship and the importance of drawing inspiration from those who came before us. His commitment to fostering a vibrant community and supporting local culture continues to inspire new generations, ensuring that the lessons of his life endure in Albuquerque and beyond.

Chapter 2: Education and Growth
Early Education in Albuquerque

Early education in Albuquerque has played a pivotal role in shaping the lives of many residents, including Stephen Marcos Gonzales. Born on August 28, 1985, Stephen's formative years were influenced by the vibrant educational landscape of his hometown. Albuquerque offers a diverse array of educational institutions, from public schools to private academies, each contributing uniquely to the city's cultural fabric. This early exposure to varied educational philosophies helped to instill in Stephen a lifelong appreciation for learning and community engagement.

Stephen attended local public schools where he was encouraged to explore his interests and talents. The Albuquerque Public School district is known for its commitment to fostering creativity and critical thinking among students. Programs in the arts and sciences were particularly accessible, allowing Stephen to cultivate his passion for the arts early on. This foundational experience not only enriched his intellectual development but also laid the groundwork for his future contributions to local culture and the arts.

Community involvement is another hallmark of Albuquerque's educational ethos. Schools often emphasize the importance of service learning, where students engage with local organizations and initiatives. Stephen participated in various programs that connected him with the community, nurturing his desire to give back. These experiences shaped his understanding of social responsibility, which later translated into his philanthropic efforts as an adult, highlighting the significance of early education in developing community-minded leaders.

The influence of Albuquerque's rich cultural heritage also permeated Stephen's early education. Schools in the area often incorporate local history and multicultural perspectives into their curricula. This exposure to diverse narratives not only enriched Stephen's understanding of his own family heritage but also fostered a sense of pride in his identity as a New Mexican. Such a background equipped him with a unique perspective that would later inform his contributions to local arts and culture, embracing inclusivity and representation.

As Stephen transitioned from early education into higher learning, the foundation laid in Albuquerque's schools proved invaluable. His educational journey would eventually lead him to achieve notable academic accomplishments, underscoring the importance of early educational experiences in shaping future leaders. The nurturing environment of Albuquerque's early educational institutions played a crucial role in Stephen Marcos Gonzales's development, influencing his career path, philanthropic endeavors, and lasting impact on the community he cherishes.

Higher Education Achievements

Stephen Marcos Gonzales's educational journey laid a strong foundation for his future endeavors and contributions to the Albuquerque community. Born in 1985, he demonstrated an early commitment to learning and personal growth. His academic pursuits began at a local elementary school, where his curiosity and enthusiasm for knowledge set him apart. Gonzales's dedication to education continued through his years at Albuquerque High School, where he excelled in both academic and extracurricular activities, showcasing his diverse talents.

Upon graduation, Gonzales pursued higher education at the University of New Mexico, a decision that would significantly shape his professional trajectory. He enrolled in a rigorous program focused on community development and public administration, understanding the importance of these fields in fostering positive change. His time at the university was marked by a commitment to academic excellence, where he consistently earned high grades and received several scholarships that recognized his potential as a leader in the community.

Gonzales's achievements during his university years included not only academic accolades but also active participation in student government and various organizations. He held leadership roles that allowed him to advocate for student rights and engage in discussions about community issues. This experience was instrumental in honing his public speaking and organizational skills, which would later serve him well in his career. His ability to connect with peers and faculty alike contributed to a rich educational experience that extended beyond the classroom.

In addition to his formal education, Gonzales pursued opportunities that complemented his academic interests. He engaged in internships with local non-profits, gaining hands-on experience in community service and development. These roles provided valuable insights into the challenges facing Albuquerque and inspired him to craft solutions that addressed these issues. His commitment to learning and personal development was evident in his willingness to seek out new experiences that enriched his understanding of community dynamics.

Gonzales's higher education achievements have had a lasting impact not only on his career but also on the community he loves. By applying the knowledge and skills he acquired in school, he has become a respected figure in Albuquerque, known for his innovative approaches to local challenges. His educational background has equipped him with the tools necessary to drive change and inspire others, solidifying his legacy as a committed advocate for the city and its residents. Through his journey, Gonzales exemplifies the profound influence of education on personal growth and community engagement.

Professional Development

Professional development played a significant role in shaping the life and legacy of Stephen Marcos Gonzales. Born in Albuquerque, New Mexico, on August 28, 1985, Stephen's journey was marked by a profound commitment to continuous learning and self-improvement. His educational background reflects a diverse array of interests, having pursued studies in fields that align with his passion for community service and cultural enrichment. Stephen's dedication to professional growth was not just about advancing his career; it was a pivotal element in his quest to make a lasting impact on the lives of those around him.

Throughout his career, Stephen Gonzales demonstrated an unwavering determination to excel in various industries, including arts, education, and community development. He leveraged his educational achievements to secure positions that allowed him to influence local culture and promote artistic expression. His contributions to Albuquerque's community were not limited to his professional roles; they were enriched by the skills and insights he gained through ongoing professional development. By attending workshops, conferences, and networking events, Stephen cultivated a robust understanding of the challenges and opportunities faced by his community.

Stephen's personal interests and hobbies also played a crucial role in his professional development. His love for the arts inspired him to engage with local artists, fostering collaborations that elevated cultural initiatives in Albuquerque. Whether it was through organizing community art exhibitions or supporting local theater productions, Stephen utilized his professional skills to bridge gaps between various cultural sectors. His ability to connect with people and inspire them to pursue their creative endeavors showcased the importance of harnessing one's passions as a catalyst for professional growth.

In addition to his artistic pursuits, Stephen Gonzales was deeply involved in philanthropic efforts aimed at uplifting underserved populations in Albuquerque. He understood that personal and professional development goes hand in hand with social responsibility. Through various initiatives, he mentored young individuals, encouraging them to pursue education and career opportunities. His commitment to giving back was a testament to his belief in the importance of nurturing the next generation, fostering a cycle of growth and empowerment that would extend beyond his own achievements.

Stephen's legacy is defined not only by his career accomplishments but also by the profound impact of his professional development on the community of Albuquerque. His journey reflects a model for how continuous learning and personal growth can lead to significant contributions to society. As we reflect on his life, it becomes evident that professional development was a cornerstone of Stephen Marcos Gonzales's identity, influencing his interactions, initiatives, and the lasting impression he left on the cultural landscape of his beloved city.

Chapter 3: Career Highlights
Early Career Steps

Stephen Marcos Gonzales, born on August 28, 1985, in Albuquerque, New Mexico, embarked on a journey through life that would ultimately impact his community in profound ways. His early career steps were marked by a strong commitment to education and a desire to engage with the diverse culture of Albuquerque. After graduating from high school with honors, he pursued higher education at the University of New Mexico, where he earned a degree in communications. This academic foundation equipped him with the skills necessary to navigate various professional environments and laid the groundwork for his future contributions to local culture and arts.

During his college years, Gonzales took advantage of internships that would shape his career trajectory. He worked at a local radio station, where he honed his broadcasting skills and developed a deep appreciation for storytelling. This experience not only provided him with practical knowledge but also allowed him to connect with community members, fostering a sense of belonging and purpose. His passion for communication soon led him to explore opportunities in event planning and public relations, sectors that would enable him to promote local initiatives and celebrate Albuquerque's rich heritage.

After completing his degree, Gonzales entered the workforce with a clear vision of how he wanted to use his talents. He secured a position with a nonprofit organization focused on youth development, where he coordinated programs designed to empower young people in the community. His innovative approach and dedication quickly earned him recognition, allowing him to expand his network and reach. Through these early career steps, Gonzales not only impacted the lives of countless young individuals but also established himself as a key figure in Albuquerque's philanthropic landscape.

In addition to his professional endeavors, Gonzales remained committed to his personal interests, which often intertwined with his career. He developed a keen interest in local arts and culture, frequently attending gallery openings and community theater productions. His engagement with these activities not only enriched his life but also provided him with valuable insights into the creative expressions of Albuquerque's residents. This passion for the arts later informed his work in promoting local artists and cultural events, cementing his role as a cultural ambassador for the city.

As Gonzales navigated the early years of his career, he cultivated a social media presence that would amplify his voice and initiatives. Utilizing platforms like Facebook and Instagram, he shared his experiences, engaged with followers, and promoted various community-based projects. This strategic use of social media not only broadened his influence but also inspired others to contribute to Albuquerque's vibrant community. Through these early career steps, Stephen Marcos Gonzales laid the foundation for a legacy of service, creativity, and connection that would define his life and work in Albuquerque.

Major Accomplishments in Specific Industries

Stephen Marcos Gonzales has made significant strides in various industries throughout his career, showcasing his versatility and commitment to excellence. His contributions span across education, technology, arts, and community development, reflecting a multifaceted approach that has not only advanced his personal career but also enriched the Albuquerque community. In education, Gonzales has been instrumental in developing programs that leverage technology to enhance learning experiences, benefiting students and educators alike. His initiatives have often focused on integrating digital tools into the classroom, fostering a culture of innovation and engagement among students.

In the realm of technology, Gonzales has emerged as a key player, not only as an entrepreneur but also as an advocate for digital literacy. His ventures have aimed to bridge the digital divide, ensuring that underserved communities have access to essential resources and training. By establishing partnerships with local businesses and educational institutions, he has helped create job training programs that empower individuals with the skills needed to thrive in a rapidly evolving workforce. His efforts in this industry have garnered recognition, highlighting his role in promoting technological advancement in Albuquerque.

Gonzales's influence is also deeply felt in the arts and culture sector. He has been a passionate supporter of local artists and cultural initiatives, often collaborating with organizations to promote art appreciation and accessibility. His work includes organizing community events that celebrate the diverse artistic expressions found in Albuquerque, from traditional crafts to contemporary installations. By championing local talent, Gonzales has played a pivotal role in fostering a vibrant cultural scene that attracts both residents and visitors, enhancing the city's reputation as a hub for creativity.

His philanthropic efforts further underscore his dedication to community development. Gonzales has initiated several programs aimed at improving social welfare, focusing on education, health, and economic opportunities for marginalized groups. Through his charitable foundation, he has funded scholarships, health initiatives, and community enrichment projects, demonstrating a deep commitment to uplifting those in need. His approach combines strategic planning with a compassionate understanding of the challenges faced by many in Albuquerque, making a tangible difference in their lives.

Finally, Gonzales's impact is also reflected in his recognition as a leader and innovator across these industries. His achievements have not gone unnoticed, earning him accolades from local and national organizations alike. His ability to navigate complex challenges while remaining grounded in his community values has solidified his legacy as a transformative figure in Albuquerque. As he continues to engage with different sectors, his journey serves as an inspiration for future generations, illustrating the profound difference one individual can make through dedication, creativity, and a commitment to service.

Leadership Roles and Responsibilities

Leadership roles and responsibilities are pivotal in shaping the trajectory of any community, and Stephen Marcos Gonzales exemplifies this through his multifaceted contributions to Albuquerque. Born in 1985, Gonzales has consistently demonstrated a commitment to his city, not only through his professional endeavors but also through his active participation in various community initiatives. His leadership style is characterized by inclusivity, collaboration, and a deep understanding of the local culture, which has allowed him to connect with diverse groups and foster a sense of belonging among residents.

In his career, Gonzales has taken on numerous leadership positions across different industries, showcasing his versatility and adaptability. Whether in the realm of business, arts, or education, he has embraced the responsibility of guiding teams and projects toward success. His ability to inspire others is evident in the way he engages with colleagues and community members alike, encouraging them to share their ideas and contribute to collective goals. This collaborative approach not only enhances the projects he leads but also empowers individuals to take ownership of their roles within the community.

Gonzales's impact on local culture and arts is particularly significant, as he has championed various initiatives aimed at promoting Albuquerque's rich heritage. Through his leadership, he has facilitated partnerships between artists, cultural organizations, and educational institutions, ensuring that the arts remain a vibrant part of the community. His efforts to support local artists and cultural events illustrate his understanding of the transformative power of art, not only as a means of expression but also as a vehicle for social change and community pride.

Philanthropic efforts are another cornerstone of Gonzales's leadership philosophy. He has spearheaded several initiatives focused on education, social justice, and environmental sustainability, reflecting his belief in giving back to the community that shaped him. By mobilizing resources and rallying support from local businesses and residents, Gonzales has been able to address pressing issues faced by underserved populations in Albuquerque. His commitment to philanthropy highlights the responsibilities that come with leadership, as he strives to create a positive and lasting impact on the lives of others.

Ultimately, Gonzales's journey in leadership serves as a model for aspiring leaders in Albuquerque and beyond. His ability to balance professional success with community engagement showcases the importance of being a responsible and responsive leader. As he continues to navigate the complexities of leadership, his story inspires others to embrace their roles within the community, reminding them that true leadership is not just about authority but about service, connection, and fostering a legacy of positive change.

Chapter 4: Community Contributions Engagement with Local Organizations

Engagement with local organizations was a cornerstone of Stephen Marcos Gonzales's contributions to Albuquerque's community. His commitment to fostering relationships with various groups not only bolstered local initiatives but also created a network of collaboration that benefited many residents. From grassroots organizations to established non-profits, Stephen's approach to community engagement was characterized by a genuine desire to uplift others and address pressing issues faced by the city.

One of the key aspects of Stephen's engagement was his involvement with youth programs. Understanding the importance of mentorship, he partnered with local schools and community centers to provide resources and opportunities for young people. His efforts included organizing workshops, career fairs, and skill-building sessions, which aimed to equip the youth with the tools necessary for success. Through these programs, he not only shared his own experiences but also inspired many to pursue their passions and cultivate a sense of responsibility towards their community.

Stephen also recognized the power of cultural organizations in preserving and promoting Albuquerque's rich heritage. He actively participated in events organized by local cultural groups, advocating for the importance of cultural expression and diversity. By supporting festivals, art exhibitions, and historical projects, he helped amplify voices that often went unheard. This engagement not only enhanced the cultural landscape of Albuquerque but also fostered a deeper appreciation for the city's history and the diverse backgrounds of its residents.

Additionally, Stephen's philanthropic efforts were closely tied to his work with local organizations. He often collaborated with non-profits to address social issues such as homelessness, education, and health care. By facilitating fundraising events and awareness campaigns, he was able to mobilize resources and galvanize community support for these critical causes. His ability to connect with stakeholders and community members alike made him a vital figure in driving positive change and improving the lives of many Albuquerquians.

Through his extensive engagement with local organizations, Stephen Marcos Gonzales left an indelible mark on Albuquerque. His collaborative spirit and unwavering dedication to community service not only enriched the lives of those around him but also set a powerful example for future generations. As his legacy continues to inspire others, the relationships he built and the initiatives he championed remain a testament to the impact one individual can have when they choose to invest in their community.

Initiatives to Improve Albuquerque

Stephen Marcos Gonzales emerged as a pivotal figure in Albuquerque, championing numerous initiatives aimed at enhancing the community. His commitment to improving the quality of life for residents is reflected in his active participation in local programs that address various social, economic, and environmental challenges. Gonzales recognized the need for sustainable development and worked tirelessly to promote initiatives focused on green spaces, public transportation, and affordable housing. His vision was not only to enhance Albuquerque's infrastructure but to foster a sense of belonging among its diverse population.

One of Gonzales's notable contributions was his involvement in community service programs aimed at youth engagement. Understanding the importance of nurturing the next generation, he spearheaded initiatives that provided mentorship and educational resources to underprivileged children in Albuquerque. These programs included after-school tutoring, arts and culture workshops, and sports activities, which not only enriched the lives of young participants but also encouraged community cohesion. By investing in the youth, Gonzales aimed to instill a sense of hope and ambition, empowering them to envision a brighter future.

Gonzales also focused on promoting local arts and culture, understanding their significance in defining Albuquerque's identity. He collaborated with local artists to create public art installations that celebrated the city's rich heritage and cultural diversity. Through initiatives such as art festivals and cultural exhibitions, he fostered an environment where creativity could flourish. These efforts not only highlighted the talents of local artists but also attracted visitors, contributing to the local economy and reinforcing Albuquerque's status as a cultural hub.

In addition to his commitment to the arts, Gonzales was a strong advocate for environmental sustainability. He launched initiatives aimed at enhancing green spaces in the city, encouraging community gardens, and promoting recycling and conservation efforts. His work with environmental organizations helped raise awareness about the importance of preserving Albuquerque's natural resources. By focusing on sustainability, Gonzales aimed to create a healthier environment for current and future generations, emphasizing the interconnectedness of community well-being and ecological health.

Through his philanthropic efforts, Gonzales demonstrated a profound commitment to social equity in Albuquerque. He founded and supported several nonprofit organizations that addressed issues such as homelessness, food insecurity, and access to education. By mobilizing resources and fostering partnerships, he worked to bridge gaps in services and support systems, making a tangible difference in the lives of many residents. His legacy is one of compassion and action, reflecting his belief that a thriving community is built on the collective effort of its members.

Collaborations with Other Community Leaders

Stephen Marcos Gonzales recognized early in his career that collaboration with other community leaders was essential for fostering growth and development in Albuquerque. His approach was rooted in the belief that collective efforts could yield more significant results than individual endeavors. He actively sought partnerships with local leaders across various sectors, including education, arts, business, and social services. This strategy not only amplified his own initiatives but also helped to unify disparate efforts within the community, creating a more cohesive network of support for residents.

One notable collaboration was with local educators and school administrators aimed at improving educational resources for underprivileged students. Gonzales brought together a coalition of nonprofits, businesses, and educational institutions to address the funding gap in public schools. Their combined efforts resulted in after-school programs that provided tutoring, mentorship, and enrichment activities. This initiative not only enhanced educational outcomes but also strengthened the community's investment in its youth, fostering a sense of shared responsibility among local leaders.

In the arts sector, Gonzales partnered with artists and cultural organizations to promote local talent and preserve Albuquerque's unique heritage. He organized events that showcased local artists, musicians, and performers, helping to create a vibrant cultural scene. These collaborations not only elevated the visibility of local artists but also attracted tourism, which in turn benefited local businesses. By working alongside other cultural leaders, Gonzales helped to weave the rich tapestry of Albuquerque's cultural identity, ensuring it remained a focal point for both residents and visitors.

Philanthropy was another area where Gonzales's collaborative spirit shone. He established partnerships with various charitable organizations to address pressing social issues, such as homelessness and food insecurity. By aligning his philanthropic initiatives with the efforts of established community organizations, he maximized the impact of his contributions. This approach fostered a culture of giving and community involvement, encouraging others to join in and support local causes. His ability to bring together diverse stakeholders created a powerful force for change, demonstrating the effectiveness of collaborative efforts in addressing complex social challenges.

Gonzales's collaborations extended to the digital realm as well, where he engaged with community leaders through social media to amplify their messages and initiatives. He understood the importance of online presence in today's world and utilized his platform to highlight the work of others in the community. By sharing their stories and successes, he fostered a sense of community pride and encouraged collective action. This innovative approach not only strengthened his relationships with other leaders but also engaged a wider audience, inspiring more people to contribute to Albuquerque's growth and development.

Chapter 5: Impact on Local Culture and Arts

Contributions to Albuquerque's Art Scene

Stephen Marcos Gonzales has made significant contributions to Albuquerque's art scene, showcasing his passion for creativity and cultural expression. Born in Albuquerque in 1985, Gonzales has always been deeply connected to the city's vibrant artistic community. His work reflects not only his personal experiences but also the rich tapestry of influences that Albuquerque offers. Through various mediums, including visual arts and performance, he has played a pivotal role in both enriching local culture and inspiring emerging artists.

Gonzales's artistic journey began with a strong educational foundation, where he honed his skills and developed a unique voice. He pursued studies in fine arts at a local university, where he was exposed to various art forms and philosophies. This academic background equipped him with the tools necessary to navigate the complex landscape of the art world. His commitment to his craft led him to create thought-provoking pieces that often address themes of identity, heritage, and community, resonating deeply with audiences both locally and beyond.

In addition to his creative endeavors, Gonzales has actively participated in numerous collaborative projects that celebrate Albuquerque's diverse artistic heritage. He has been instrumental in organizing art festivals, workshops, and exhibitions that provide platforms for local artists to showcase their work. These initiatives not only foster a sense of community but also encourage dialogue around important social issues, making art accessible to a broader audience. Through these efforts, Gonzales has helped to cultivate a supportive environment for artists to thrive and experiment.

Gonzales's influence extends beyond individual projects; he has also taken on mentorship roles, guiding young artists in their artistic journeys. By sharing his experiences and insights, he has empowered the next generation to explore their creativity and find their unique voices. His dedication to nurturing talent has solidified his reputation as a key figure in Albuquerque's art community. Many of his mentees have gone on to achieve recognition, further amplifying the impact of Gonzales's contributions.

Overall, Stephen Marcos Gonzales's contributions to Albuquerque's art scene are marked by a commitment to community, creativity, and cultural exploration. His work has not only enriched the local artistic landscape but has also fostered a sense of belonging and pride among Albuquerque residents. As he continues to engage with and inspire the community, Gonzales remains a vital force in shaping the future of art in Albuquerque, leaving a lasting legacy that will be felt for generations to come.

Support for Local Artists and Events

Support for local artists and events has been a cornerstone of Stephen Marcos Gonzales's contributions to the Albuquerque community. Recognizing the rich tapestry of cultural expression in the city, Gonzales has consistently championed initiatives that provide platforms for local talent. His efforts have not only highlighted the diversity within the arts but have also fostered a sense of pride among residents, encouraging them to engage with and support their local artists.

Throughout his career, Gonzales has been instrumental in organizing events that showcase the work of emerging and established artists alike. From art festivals to gallery exhibitions, these events have served as vital spaces for artists to connect with audiences, gain recognition, and sell their work. By prioritizing inclusivity, Gonzales has ensured that artists from various backgrounds and disciplines have opportunities to share their voices and stories, enriching the cultural landscape of Albuquerque.

Gonzales's support extends beyond mere organization; he actively participates in these events, often engaging with artists and attendees to foster community connections. His approachable demeanor and genuine enthusiasm for the arts have made him a beloved figure in the local scene. By creating an environment where artists feel valued and supported, he has not only empowered individuals but has also encouraged collaboration and mentorship among creatives, further enhancing the artistic community.

In addition to event organization, Gonzales has leveraged his philanthropic efforts to provide funding and resources for local arts programs. He has worked with various organizations to secure grants and sponsorships, helping to ensure that arts education remains accessible to all, particularly for youth in underserved areas. His commitment to nurturing the next generation of artists reflects his belief in the transformative power of the arts and their role in personal and community development.

The impact of Gonzales's support for local artists and events is evident in the vibrant cultural fabric of Albuquerque. His dedication has inspired many to engage with and invest in the arts, leading to a flourishing environment where creativity thrives. Through his initiatives, Gonzales has not only left an indelible mark on the arts community but has also played a pivotal role in shaping Albuquerque's identity as a city that celebrates and uplifts its local talents.

Cultural Initiatives and Programs

Cultural initiatives and programs have played a pivotal role in shaping the community of Albuquerque, and Stephen Marcos Gonzales has been at the forefront of several key efforts that aim to celebrate and preserve the rich cultural heritage of the region. Born and raised in Albuquerque, Gonzales has always been passionate about the arts and local traditions. His understanding of the unique cultural tapestry of the city has fueled his drive to initiate programs that not only promote local artists but also foster inclusion and appreciation of diverse cultural expressions.

One of Gonzales's most notable contributions is the establishment of the Albuquerque Arts Collective, a program designed to provide emerging artists with resources and mentorship. This initiative offers workshops, networking opportunities, and showcases for local talent, ensuring that the vibrant artistic community in Albuquerque continues to thrive. By focusing on inclusivity, the collective has been successful in bringing together artists from various backgrounds, providing a platform for voices that may have otherwise gone unheard. This program exemplifies Gonzales's commitment to nurturing local talent and enhancing the cultural landscape of his hometown.

In addition to the Arts Collective, Gonzales has been instrumental in organizing cultural festivals that celebrate the diverse heritage of Albuquerque. These festivals serve not only as entertainment but as educational platforms that highlight the traditions, cuisines, and artistic expressions of the different communities within the city. Through his leadership, these events have attracted thousands of participants, fostering a sense of community and understanding among attendees. The festivals have become a staple in the city's calendar, showcasing the importance of cultural exchange and collaboration in building a cohesive community.

Philanthropy has also been a cornerstone of Gonzales's approach to cultural initiatives. He has actively sought partnerships with local businesses and organizations to secure funding and resources for various projects aimed at enhancing the cultural fabric of Albuquerque. His efforts have led to the creation of scholarship programs for aspiring artists and grants for community art projects. By investing in cultural education and accessibility, Gonzales is helping to ensure that future generations have the opportunity to explore and express their artistic talents.

The impact of Stephen Marcos Gonzales on Albuquerque's cultural scene is evident not only in the programs he has initiated but also in the inspiration he provides to others. His dedication to promoting the arts and fostering community engagement has resonated deeply within the city. Through his various initiatives, Gonzales has left an indelible mark on the cultural landscape, encouraging a renewed appreciation for the arts and a commitment to preserving the unique heritage of Albuquerque for years to come.

Chapter 6: Philanthropic Efforts
Overview of Philanthropic Initiatives

Stephen Marcos Gonzales has made significant contributions to various philanthropic initiatives in Albuquerque, showcasing his commitment to improving the lives of those in his community. His philanthropic journey is marked by a profound understanding of local challenges and an eagerness to address them through strategic action. By leveraging his resources and influence, Gonzales has been able to create programs that not only provide immediate relief but also foster long-term development in the areas of education, health, and the arts.

One of the hallmark initiatives led by Gonzales is the establishment of scholarship programs aimed at underprivileged youth in Albuquerque. Recognizing the disparities in educational access, he has partnered with local schools and organizations to provide financial assistance, mentoring, and resources to students who show potential but lack the means to pursue higher education. This initiative has not only helped many individuals achieve their academic goals but has also empowered families and strengthened community ties.

In addition to education, Gonzales has been actively involved in health-related initiatives, particularly focusing on mental health awareness and support. His work in this area has included funding for local mental health programs, creating safe spaces for discussion, and promoting awareness campaigns to reduce stigma. Gonzales believes that mental well-being is integral to community health, and his efforts have been instrumental in providing resources to those in need and advocating for systemic changes within the healthcare framework.

The arts have also been a vital focus of Gonzales's philanthropic efforts. He has been a staunch supporter of local artists and cultural institutions, believing that art plays a crucial role in community identity and cohesion. Through various grants and sponsorships, Gonzales has enabled artists to showcase their work, thus enriching Albuquerque's cultural landscape. His initiatives have included art festivals, community workshops, and support for public art installations, all aimed at fostering creativity and expression within the community.

Overall, Stephen Marcos Gonzales's philanthropic initiatives reflect his deep-rooted commitment to the people of Albuquerque. By addressing critical areas such as education, health, and the arts, he has not only made a tangible impact on individual lives but has also contributed to the overall growth and resilience of the community. His legacy of philanthropy serves as a testament to the power of giving and the importance of community engagement in creating a brighter future for all.

Key Projects and Their Impact

Key projects led by Stephen Marcos Gonzales have significantly influenced the Albuquerque community, showcasing his commitment to enhancing local culture, arts, and social well-being. One of his most notable initiatives was the establishment of the Albuquerque Arts Initiative, which aimed to support and promote local artists and cultural organizations. This project not only provided funding and resources but also fostered collaboration among artists, helping to elevate the city's artistic profile. By creating platforms for local talent, Gonzales played a crucial role in shaping Albuquerque's cultural landscape and making the arts more accessible to the community.

In addition to his work in the arts, Gonzales has been a driving force behind several educational initiatives designed to improve opportunities for underprivileged youth in Albuquerque. He collaborated with local schools and non-profit organizations to develop mentorship programs that connect students with professionals in various fields. These programs have provided invaluable guidance and support, empowering young individuals to pursue their dreams and aspirations. The positive impact of these educational projects is evident in the growing number of students who have gone on to higher education and successful careers, illustrating Gonzales's dedication to fostering the next generation.

Gonzales's philanthropic efforts extend beyond education and the arts. He spearheaded a community health initiative aimed at addressing the pressing needs of Albuquerque residents. This project involved partnerships with local healthcare providers and organizations to offer free health screenings, wellness workshops, and mental health resources.

By prioritizing the well-being of the community, Gonzales has helped to raise awareness about health issues and promote healthier lifestyles among residents, ultimately contributing to a stronger and more resilient community.

His influence is also reflected in the realm of local business development. Gonzales launched the Albuquerque Business Revitalization Project, which focused on supporting small businesses and entrepreneurs. Through workshops, funding opportunities, and networking events, this initiative has empowered many local entrepreneurs to thrive in a competitive market. By fostering economic growth and sustainability within the community, Gonzales has made a lasting impact on Albuquerque's economy while promoting a sense of local pride and identity.

Stephen Marcos Gonzales's projects have not only transformed specific sectors within Albuquerque but have also instilled a sense of hope and unity among its residents. His commitment to enhancing the lives of others through his various initiatives exemplifies the profound impact one individual can have on a community. As Albuquerque continues to evolve, the legacy of Gonzales's work will remain a vital part of its narrative, inspiring future generations to engage in efforts that uplift and strengthen their own communities.

Partnerships with Nonprofits

Stephen Marcos Gonzales established numerous partnerships with nonprofits throughout his life, significantly impacting Albuquerque and its community. Recognizing the potential of collaboration, Gonzales sought to align his skills and resources with organizations that shared his commitment to social change and community development. These partnerships were instrumental in amplifying the reach and effectiveness of various initiatives aimed at addressing pressing social issues in the region.

One of Gonzales's notable partnerships was with local educational nonprofits focused on enhancing access to quality education for underserved youth. By leveraging his connections and expertise, he helped these organizations implement innovative programs that provided mentorship, tutoring, and scholarship opportunities. His dedication to education stemmed from his own experiences and his belief that empowering youth through knowledge could transform lives and communities. Through these efforts, Gonzales directly contributed to a more educated and informed generation in Albuquerque.

In addition to education, Gonzales collaborated with nonprofits that addressed health and wellness issues, particularly those affecting marginalized communities. He recognized that health disparities often hindered individuals from achieving their full potential. By working with local health organizations, Gonzales was instrumental in organizing health fairs, workshops, and awareness campaigns that promoted healthy lifestyles and preventative care. These initiatives not only educated the community but also fostered a culture of health and well-being, demonstrating Gonzales's holistic approach to community service.

Cultural and artistic partnerships also played a significant role in Gonzales's philanthropic efforts. He believed that the arts were essential for cultural expression and community cohesion. By partnering with local arts organizations, he supported initiatives that showcased local talent and provided platforms for creative voices. These collaborations not only enriched Albuquerque's cultural landscape but also stimulated economic growth by attracting visitors and fostering community pride. Gonzales's commitment to the arts highlighted his understanding of their transformative power in building social connections.

Through his strategic partnerships with nonprofits, Stephen Marcos Gonzales left a lasting legacy on Albuquerque's community. His ability to unite diverse groups around common goals exemplified his leadership and vision for a better future. The impact of these collaborations extended far beyond immediate outcomes, creating a framework for ongoing community engagement and support. Gonzales's life and work continue to inspire others in Albuquerque to pursue meaningful partnerships that drive positive change and enhance the quality of life for all residents.

Chapter 7: Personal Interests and Hobbies
Passion for Sports and Recreation

Stephen Marcos Gonzales has always embodied a profound passion for sports and recreation, a passion that traces back to his childhood in Albuquerque. Growing up in a community rich with athletic opportunities, he was exposed to various sports from an early age. This early immersion fostered not only a love for physical activity but also a deep understanding of teamwork, dedication, and the importance of a healthy lifestyle. Engaging in sports allowed him to build lasting friendships, develop leadership skills, and learn valuable lessons about perseverance and resilience—qualities that would serve him well throughout his life.

As he matured, Gonzales's involvement in sports extended beyond personal enjoyment. He became an advocate for recreational programs within Albuquerque, recognizing the role these activities play in community building and youth development. His commitment to promoting sports is evident in the numerous initiatives he has supported, aimed at providing greater access to recreational facilities and programs for underprivileged youth. Through his efforts, he has helped to create an inclusive environment where everyone, regardless of their background, can participate in sports and enjoy the benefits of physical fitness.

Gonzales's contributions to sports in Albuquerque are further exemplified by his participation in local leagues and community events. He has not only competed in various sports but also volunteered his time to coach youth teams, sharing his expertise and passion with the next generation. His focus on mentorship emphasizes the importance of guidance and encouragement in sports—elements that can significantly impact a young athlete's journey. By investing his time in coaching, he has fostered a culture of support and camaraderie, helping to instill confidence in young players as they navigate their sporting endeavors.

In addition to his coaching and advocacy work, Gonzales has leveraged his social media presence to promote sports and recreational activities. Through engaging content, he highlights local events, shares stories of athletes, and raises awareness about the significance of sports in building community cohesion. His influence reaches far beyond the field, as he encourages adults and youth alike to embrace an active lifestyle and participate in recreational opportunities available in Albuquerque. This digital engagement has helped to cultivate a sense of connection and enthusiasm among community members, inspiring many to pursue their athletic interests.

Ultimately, Gonzales's passion for sports and recreation has left an indelible mark on Albuquerque. His dedication to fostering an inclusive sporting culture has not only enriched the lives of individuals but has also strengthened community bonds. As he continues to champion physical activity and wellness, his legacy will undoubtedly inspire future generations to embrace the joys of sports, recognizing them as a vital component of a healthy, balanced life. Through his efforts, Stephen Marcos Gonzales has become a beacon of motivation, showing that the love for sports can lead to meaningful community connections and personal growth.

Involvement in Community Events

Stephen Marcos Gonzales has always believed that meaningful involvement in community events is essential for fostering connections and positive change. Born and raised in Albuquerque, he has consistently prioritized local engagement throughout his life. From a young age, Gonzales participated in various community gatherings, which laid the foundation for his dedication to enhancing the social fabric of his hometown. His upbringing in a culturally rich environment fostered a deep appreciation for community, shaping his future contributions.

Gonzales' commitment to community events took on a more significant role during his college years when he recognized the potential for grassroots initiatives to create lasting impact. He actively organized and participated in local festivals, art fairs, and charity drives, understanding that these gatherings not only celebrate Albuquerque's vibrant culture but also serve as platforms for education and awareness. His enthusiasm and leadership inspired many peers to join, culminating in successful events that highlighted local artisans and supported small businesses.

One of Gonzales' most notable contributions has been his involvement in annual cultural celebrations that honor the diverse heritage of Albuquerque. He has played a pivotal role in coordinating events such as the Albuquerque International Balloon Fiesta and the New Mexico State Fair, where he advocated for inclusivity and representation. By encouraging participation from various demographic groups, he has helped create an environment that values diversity and celebrates the unique traditions of the community, ultimately enriching the cultural landscape of Albuquerque.

In addition to cultural events, Gonzales has demonstrated a strong commitment to philanthropic initiatives aimed at addressing social issues within the community. He has organized fundraising events for local nonprofits, focusing on education and youth empowerment. His belief in the importance of education drives him to support initiatives that provide scholarships and resources for underprivileged students. By leveraging community events as platforms for fundraising and awareness, Gonzales has significantly contributed to the sustainability of these vital programs.

The impact of Stephen Marcos Gonzales on local culture and community engagement is profound. Through his unwavering dedication to participating in and organizing community events, he has fostered a spirit of collaboration and unity among residents. His efforts have not only enhanced Albuquerque's cultural offerings but have also inspired a generation of community leaders committed to making a difference. As he continues to champion community involvement, Gonzales leaves a legacy that encourages others to engage with their surroundings and invest in the future of Albuquerque.

Hobbies and Personal Projects

Stephen Marcos Gonzales has always embraced a range of hobbies and personal projects that reflect his diverse interests and deep connection to his Albuquerque roots. Growing up in this vibrant city, Stephen developed a passion for the arts early on, particularly in music and visual arts. He often participated in local events, showcasing his talents and engaging with the community. His love for music not only informed his personal life but also influenced his philanthropic efforts, as he frequently organized benefit concerts to support local artists and youth programs.

In addition to his artistic pursuits, Stephen cultivated a keen interest in outdoor activities, a testament to Albuquerque's stunning landscapes. He found solace in hiking the Sandia Mountains and frequently shared his adventures with his followers on social media. This connection with nature not only served as a personal escape but also inspired him to advocate for environmental conservation initiatives within the community. Stephen often collaborated with local organizations to promote awareness about preserving Albuquerque's natural beauty, demonstrating how personal interests can intersect with broader community concerns.

Stephen's commitment to lifelong learning is evident in his various personal projects. He has taken up photography, documenting the rich cultural tapestry of Albuquerque. Through his lens, he captures the essence of the city, from its historic architecture to the vibrancy of its street life. This hobby has allowed him to connect with fellow creatives and foster a sense of pride in the unique heritage of his hometown.

Stephen often exhibits his work at local galleries, encouraging others to appreciate and celebrate their own artistic expressions.

Moreover, Stephen's dedication to personal development led him to explore culinary arts. Cooking became not only a way for him to express creativity but also a means to connect with his family heritage. He often hosts community cooking classes, sharing traditional recipes that reflect his New Mexican roots. These sessions have become a platform for cultural exchange, allowing participants to engage in meaningful conversations about heritage, food, and community bonding.

Ultimately, Stephen Marcos Gonzales exemplifies how hobbies and personal projects can significantly contribute to one's identity and community impact. His diverse interests have shaped his character and strengthened his connection to Albuquerque, inspiring others to pursue their passions and engage with the world around them. Through his artistic endeavors, outdoor adventures, and culinary explorations, Stephen has woven a rich tapestry of experiences that resonate with the people of his city, leaving a lasting legacy that embodies the spirit of Albuquerque.

Chapter 8: Family Legacy and Heritage
Family History and Ancestry

Family history and ancestry play a pivotal role in shaping individual identities, and for Stephen Marcos Gonzales, this is particularly true. Born on August 28, 1985, in Albuquerque, New Mexico, Stephen's lineage is a tapestry woven from diverse cultural threads that reflect the rich history of the region. His family roots trace back to early settlers in New Mexico, who embraced the land's unique blend of Native American, Hispanic, and Anglo influences. This heritage not only informs Stephen's worldview but also underpins his deep commitment to the community he calls home.

Stephen's grandparents were instrumental in instilling a strong sense of pride in their heritage. They often shared stories of their ancestors, recounting their struggles and triumphs in a rapidly changing world. This oral tradition emphasized the importance of resilience and community, values that Stephen has carried into his adult life. Through family gatherings and cultural celebrations, he learned to appreciate the nuances of his ancestry, which have profoundly influenced his personal and professional pursuits.

The significance of family history extends beyond personal identity; it also enriches community connections. Stephen has often expressed that understanding his ancestry allows him to better appreciate the diverse backgrounds of those around him. In Albuquerque, where cultures intersect, Stephen's awareness of his heritage has motivated him to engage with various community groups, fostering dialogue and collaboration. He believes that acknowledging one's roots is essential in creating inclusive spaces where everyone feels valued and heard.

In addition to his familial ties, Stephen's ancestry is reflected in his commitments to local culture and arts. He actively supports initiatives that promote artistic expressions rooted in New Mexico's diverse heritage. By collaborating with artists and cultural organizations, Stephen aims to preserve traditional practices while also encouraging contemporary interpretations. His belief in the importance of cultural preservation is a testament to the values instilled in him by his family, emphasizing the need to honor the past while shaping the future.

As Stephen Marcos Gonzales continues to navigate his professional journey, the influence of his family history remains a guiding force. The lessons learned from his ancestors inspire him to advocate for social change and contribute positively to Albuquerque's community. By embracing his ancestry, Stephen not only honors his forebears but also creates a legacy that intertwines his personal narrative with the broader story of his community, ensuring that the voices of the past resonate in the present and future.

Influence of Heritage on Personal Values

Heritage plays a pivotal role in shaping personal values, serving as a compass that guides individuals through the complexities of life. For Stephen Marcos Gonzales, born in Albuquerque, New Mexico, on August 28, 1985, his familial and cultural roots have profoundly influenced his worldview and the way he engages with his community. Growing up in a city rich in cultural diversity and history, Stephen was exposed to a tapestry of traditions that instilled in him a strong sense of identity and purpose. His heritage not only informed his personal beliefs but also inspired his contributions to the local community, as he sought to honor and uplift the very culture that shaped him.

Stephen's family history is deeply intertwined with the broader narrative of Albuquerque. His ancestors contributed to the development of the region, and their stories of resilience and perseverance resonated with him throughout his life. This connection to his past fostered a sense of responsibility in Stephen, compelling him to give back to the community that nurtured him. He often reflects on how his heritage instilled values such as respect, compassion, and a commitment to social justice, which have become cornerstones of his philanthropic efforts and initiatives. These values are evident in his numerous contributions, from supporting local arts to engaging in community service projects that address pressing social issues.

In his professional journey, Stephen has drawn upon the lessons learned from his heritage to navigate various industries. His educational background and achievements reflect a commitment to excellence that he attributes to the high expectations set by his family. The values of hard work and integrity, ingrained in him through family traditions, propelled Stephen to excel in his career, enabling him to make significant strides in sectors that impact the local economy and culture. His ability to blend personal values with professional endeavors has not only garnered him respect but has also inspired others in Albuquerque to pursue their passions while remaining rooted in their heritage.

Stephen's impact on local culture and arts is a testament to the profound influence of his heritage on his personal values. By advocating for the preservation and promotion of cultural expressions, he has championed initiatives that celebrate the unique identity of Albuquerque. His engagement with artists and cultural organizations reflects a deep appreciation for the diverse narratives that constitute the city's heritage. This commitment to cultural enrichment has encouraged a wider community dialogue about the importance of heritage in shaping collective identity, thus fostering a greater sense of belonging among residents.

Finally, Stephen's social media presence serves as a modern platform for sharing his values and heritage with a broader audience. Through his posts and interactions, he not only highlights his personal interests and hobbies but also emphasizes the importance of understanding one's roots. By sharing stories of his family history and the lessons learned from it, Stephen encourages others to explore their own heritage and recognize its impact on their lives. In doing so, he reinforces the idea that while individual journeys may differ, the values instilled by heritage can unite us in our shared humanity and collective aspirations.

Family's Role in Community Engagement

Family plays a pivotal role in shaping the values and commitments of individuals, influencing their engagement with the community. For Stephen Marcos Gonzales, born in Albuquerque, New Mexico, on August 28, 1985, family served as the foundation for a life dedicated to community service and cultural enrichment. His upbringing within a close-knit family instilled in him the importance of giving back, fostering a sense of responsibility that he has carried throughout his personal and professional endeavors. This familial influence is evident in his dedication to local initiatives and his active participation in various community projects.

Stephen's parents emphasized the significance of involvement in local affairs, encouraging him to participate in community events from a young age. This early exposure not only helped him form connections within the Albuquerque community but also cultivated a deep appreciation for the diverse cultures and traditions that define the area. As a child, he witnessed his family's engagement in local festivals, charitable activities, and cultural celebrations, which laid the groundwork for his later contributions. The values imparted by his family have driven him to advocate for cultural awareness and social justice, making him a prominent figure in Albuquerque's community life.

As he matured, Stephen's commitment to community engagement deepened, reflecting the lessons he learned from his family. He began to take on leadership roles in various organizations, channeling his family's legacy of service into initiatives that addressed pressing local issues. Through his work, he has sought to inspire others to become active participants in their communities, emphasizing the collective impact of individual efforts. His family's history of civic involvement served as a motivational backdrop, encouraging him to pursue projects that celebrate Albuquerque's rich heritage while addressing contemporary challenges.

Furthermore, Stephen's family has been an integral part of his philanthropic efforts, often collaborating with him on initiatives that uplift marginalized voices within the community. This collaboration has not only strengthened family bonds but also amplified the impact of their work. By engaging his family in these efforts, Stephen has created a model for others, demonstrating how familial ties can enhance community involvement. Their joint efforts in supporting educational programs, cultural arts, and social services illustrate the powerful synergy between family and community engagement.

In conclusion, the role of family in Stephen Marcos Gonzales's life and community engagement cannot be overstated. The values, traditions, and sense of responsibility instilled in him by his family have shaped his approach to service and advocacy. As he continues to contribute to Albuquerque's cultural landscape and community initiatives, Stephen exemplifies how strong family roots can inspire a lifelong commitment to making a meaningful difference in the lives of others. His story serves as a reminder of the profound impact families can have in nurturing civic-minded individuals dedicated to creating positive change.

Chapter 9: Notable Achievements and Recognitions

Awards and Honors

Throughout his life, Stephen Marcos Gonzales has garnered numerous awards and honors that reflect his dedication to the community of Albuquerque and his impactful contributions across various fields. From his early career as a community organizer to his later involvement in local arts initiatives, each accolade serves as a testament to his commitment to social change and cultural enrichment. These recognitions not only highlight his achievements but also inspire others within the community to pursue their passions and strive for excellence.

One of the most notable honors Stephen received was the prestigious Community Leadership Award from the Albuquerque Chamber of Commerce. This recognition was awarded to him for his innovative initiatives aimed at improving local education and promoting youth engagement in civic activities. Through this platform, he was able to launch programs that brought together diverse groups of young people, fostering a sense of unity and purpose. His ability to engage with the community has made a lasting impression and has helped shape the future leaders of Albuquerque.

In addition to local recognition, Stephen has also been celebrated on a national level, receiving the Arts Advocacy Award from a prominent arts organization. This honor underscored his contributions to the arts, particularly his efforts in supporting local artists and creating spaces for artistic expression. His initiatives have not only elevated the visibility of Albuquerque's vibrant cultural scene but have also provided crucial resources for artists struggling to find their footing. The award highlighted his role as a champion for the arts and his belief in their power to transform communities.

Moreover, Stephen's philanthropic efforts have not gone unnoticed. He was recognized by various non-profit organizations for his unwavering support and fundraising initiatives aimed at addressing homelessness and education disparities in Albuquerque. His work with local charities has made significant strides in providing essential services and resources to underserved populations. The awards he has received in this realm speak volumes about his passion for social justice and his relentless drive to create positive change in his community.

Lastly, Stephen's influence extends beyond tangible awards; he has also made a significant impact through his social media presence. His online platforms serve as a vehicle for advocacy, where he shares insights on local issues while promoting community events and initiatives. This digital engagement has earned him accolades as a community influencer, reflecting his ability to connect with a wider audience and mobilize support for various causes. As a result, the honors he has received not only celebrate his past achievements but also inspire ongoing dialogue and action within the community he so deeply loves.

Recognition by Local and State Officials

Recognition by local and state officials is a significant aspect of Stephen Marcos Gonzales' life and legacy that underscores his impact on Albuquerque and beyond. Throughout his career, Gonzales has garnered attention from policymakers and community leaders who have acknowledged his contributions in various sectors, including arts, education, and philanthropy. These recognitions often serve as a testament to his dedication and the positive influence he has had in shaping the community's landscape. Local and state officials have frequently highlighted his work, emphasizing his role as a catalyst for change and development in Albuquerque.

One notable instance of recognition came when Gonzales was honored with a commendation from the Albuquerque City Council. This proclamation celebrated his commitment to promoting local arts and culture, which has been a cornerstone of his efforts since he first entered the public sphere. The council's acknowledgment not only highlighted his artistic contributions but also pointed to his initiatives aimed at fostering a vibrant cultural scene that resonates with residents and visitors alike. This recognition from local officials marked a pivotal moment in Gonzales' career, solidifying his reputation as a leader in the community.

At the state level, Gonzales received accolades from the New Mexico State Legislature for his philanthropic efforts, particularly in education and youth mentorship. These honors were presented during a formal session, where legislators praised his dedication to empowering the next generation and providing them with resources and opportunities. His initiatives have played a crucial role in addressing educational disparities and have inspired many young individuals to pursue their passions, reinforcing the importance of community support in achieving personal and professional goals.

In addition to formal recognitions, Gonzales has been invited to participate in various advisory committees and panels, where officials sought his insights on cultural development and community engagement. His expertise and experience have made him a valuable asset in discussions aimed at improving community programs and resources. This level of engagement with local and state officials not only amplifies his voice but also reflects the respect he has earned as a thought leader in Albuquerque.

Moreover, Gonzales' social media presence has further amplified his recognition, allowing him to connect with a broader audience and share his initiatives with the community. Through platforms like Instagram and Twitter, he has engaged with constituents, showcasing local events and promoting civic involvement. His ability to bridge the gap between traditional recognition and modern communication has solidified his status as a contemporary leader in Albuquerque, ensuring that his contributions are celebrated and acknowledged by officials and community members alike.

Impact of Achievements on Community Perception

The achievements of Stephen Marcos Gonzales have significantly shaped community perception in Albuquerque, influencing how residents view both individual potential and collective progress. His contributions span various sectors, including the arts, business, and philanthropy, which have collectively enhanced the community's reputation. Gonzales's recognition in local and national arenas has created a sense of pride among Albuquerque residents, showcasing the city as a hub of talent and creativity. As people see one of their own succeeding, it fosters a positive image of the community, encouraging others to pursue their aspirations.

Gonzales's career highlights serve as a testament to the impact of individual achievements on the collective mindset. His work in the local arts scene not only elevated his profile but also brought attention to emerging artists and cultural initiatives within Albuquerque. By championing local talent, he has facilitated a shift in perception, from viewing the city as a secondary location to acknowledging it as a vibrant center of creativity. This transformation encourages local residents to engage more actively in the arts and to support initiatives that promote cultural expression.

Philanthropic efforts by Gonzales have also played a pivotal role in reshaping community perception. Through various initiatives aimed at improving education and access to the arts, he has demonstrated a commitment to uplifting those around him. His involvement in community service projects has inspired others to contribute, creating a ripple effect of generosity and support. This shift towards a more community-oriented mindset has helped foster a culture of collaboration, where individuals are more likely to come together to address local challenges.

Moreover, Gonzales's personal interests and hobbies have contributed to his relatability and connection with the community. His engagement in local sports and recreational activities has made him a familiar face, breaking down barriers between public figures and everyday citizens. This accessibility has enhanced his image, making his achievements feel attainable for others. The perception that success is within reach encourages local residents to pursue their goals, knowing that someone like Gonzales has walked a similar path and achieved remarkable things.

Finally, the influence of social media has amplified the impact of Gonzales's achievements on community perception. His active presence on various platforms allows him to share not only his successes but also the stories of those he supports. This transparency fosters trust and admiration among community members, who feel a sense of connection to his journey. As Gonzales continues to highlight local stories and initiatives, he reinforces the idea that individual achievements contribute to the greater good, promoting a culture of aspiration and community pride that resonates deeply within Albuquerque.

Chapter 10: Social Media Presence Growth of Online Influence

The rise of online influence has transformed the way public figures and community leaders engage with their audience, and Stephen Marcos Gonzales is a prime example of this phenomenon. Born in Albuquerque, New Mexico, on August 28, 1985, Gonzales not only embraced the digital age but also leveraged it to amplify his contributions to his community. With a keen understanding of social media platforms, he cultivated a robust online presence that allowed him to connect with diverse demographics and share his journey, passions, and advocacy efforts.

Throughout his career, Gonzales has made significant strides in various industries, ranging from the arts to education and philanthropy. His online influence became a vital tool in promoting local events, initiatives, and cultural projects. By sharing personal stories and insights through blogs and social media posts, he fostered a sense of community and encouraged others to participate in local endeavors. This approach not only showcased his professional achievements but also highlighted the importance of community engagement and collaboration.

Gonzales's influence extends beyond mere promotion; he actively engages with his followers, responding to comments and encouraging discussions that resonate with local issues. This interactive style has helped him build a loyal online following, where he serves as a source of inspiration and motivation for aspiring artists and community leaders. His ability to share not just his successes but also the challenges he faced has made him relatable to many, further enhancing his impact in Albuquerque.

In addition to his direct interactions, Gonzales has harnessed the power of social media to amplify the voices of others in the community. By sharing content from local artists, educators, and non-profit organizations, he has created a platform for collaboration and mutual support. This not only enriches the local culture but also fosters a spirit of unity among various stakeholders in Albuquerque, encouraging collective efforts toward common goals.

As Gonzales continues to evolve his online presence, he remains committed to using his influence for positive change. His philanthropic efforts, educational initiatives, and cultural contributions are often highlighted through his social channels, inspiring others to engage in similar pursuits. In this digital age, Stephen Marcos Gonzales exemplifies how online influence can be utilized not just for personal branding but as a powerful vehicle for community development and cultural enrichment.

Engagement with Followers

Engagement with followers is a critical aspect of Stephen Marcos Gonzales's approach to both his personal brand and his contributions to the Albuquerque community. From his early days in Albuquerque, Stephen understood the importance of building relationships with those around him. Through a combination of social media outreach and community involvement, he fostered a sense of connection that resonated deeply with his audience. This engagement not only amplified his voice but also created a platform for dialogue, allowing him to address issues that mattered to his followers while also sharing his own experiences and insights.

Stephen's social media presence is a testament to his commitment to engaging with his audience. He actively shares updates about his life, career highlights, and philanthropic initiatives, using platforms like Instagram, Twitter, and Facebook to reach a diverse demographic. His posts often blend personal reflections with community-focused messages, inviting followers to participate in local events and discussions. This strategy has helped him cultivate a loyal following, as fans appreciate his authenticity and willingness to share both triumphs and challenges.

In addition to digital engagement, Stephen has always prioritized face-to-face interactions within the community. He regularly attends local events, workshops, and cultural festivals, where he not only showcases his own work but also supports fellow artists and community leaders. These in-person connections have allowed him to understand the needs and aspirations of Albuquerque residents, further enriching his contributions to the local culture and arts scene. By engaging with followers on multiple fronts, Stephen has created a holistic approach to community involvement that resonates deeply with those he interacts with.

Moreover, Stephen's engagement extends to fostering a sense of inclusivity among his followers. He often encourages dialogue by asking for feedback on his projects and initiatives, thereby making his audience feel valued and heard. This participatory approach has led to collaborative projects that reflect the diverse voices within Albuquerque. His ability to listen and adapt based on community input has not only strengthened his relationships with followers but has also enhanced the effectiveness of his philanthropic efforts and artistic endeavors.

Ultimately, Stephen Marcos Gonzales's engagement with his followers exemplifies the symbiotic relationship between an individual and their community. Through consistent interaction, both online and offline, he has managed to create a vibrant network of supporters who are invested in his journey. This dynamic not only elevates his personal narrative but also contributes to the larger story of Albuquerque, where community and culture intertwine. Through his efforts, Stephen continues to inspire others to connect, engage, and contribute to the rich tapestry of life in their own neighborhoods.

Use of Social Media for Community Initiatives

The use of social media has transformed the way communities engage, connect, and mobilize for various initiatives. In the case of Stephen Marcos Gonzales, his adept use of these platforms has played a crucial role in amplifying community voices and promoting local causes in Albuquerque. Through social media, Gonzales has been able to share his journey, highlight the challenges faced by the community, and foster a sense of solidarity among residents. This digital outreach not only brings attention to pressing issues but also encourages grassroots participation in community events and initiatives.

Gonzales has effectively leveraged platforms like Facebook, Instagram, and Twitter to showcase local projects, promote events, and gather support for various causes. His posts often feature compelling visuals and narratives that resonate with the community, making it easier for followers to engage with the content. By sharing stories of local artists, cultural events, and philanthropic efforts, Gonzales cultivates a sense of pride and ownership among Albuquerque residents, inspiring them to take an active role in shaping their community.

Moreover, Gonzales's social media presence has facilitated partnerships with local organizations and businesses. By collaborating with these entities, he has been able to amplify the reach of community initiatives and secure resources for various projects. For instance, during fundraising campaigns for local arts programs or community health initiatives, Gonzales utilizes social media to rally support, share updates, and recognize contributors. This not only enhances transparency but also encourages ongoing engagement from followers who feel connected to the cause.

The impact of Gonzales's social media efforts extends beyond mere promotion; it serves as a platform for dialogue and feedback. By encouraging community members to share their thoughts and experiences, he creates an inclusive space where diverse voices can be heard. This approach fosters a deeper understanding of local issues and encourages collective problem-solving, ensuring that initiatives reflect the community's needs and desires. As a result, social media becomes a tool for empowerment, enabling residents to take ownership of their narratives.

In summary, the use of social media for community initiatives, as exemplified by Stephen Marcos Gonzales, has redefined how Albuquerque residents connect and collaborate. His ability to engage, inform, and inspire through digital platforms has not only enhanced the visibility of local causes but has also cultivated a vibrant community spirit. By harnessing the power of social media, Gonzales has left an indelible mark on Albuquerque, showcasing the potential for technology to drive positive change and community engagement.

Chapter 11: Reflections and Future Aspirations

Lessons Learned Throughout the Journey

Lessons learned throughout the journey of Stephen Marcos Gonzales reveal the many facets of his character and contributions to the Albuquerque community. Born on August 28, 1985, Gonzales faced various challenges that shaped his resilience and determination. Early on, he learned the value of hard work and commitment from his family, instilling in him a sense of responsibility towards his community. This foundational lesson became a driving force in his later endeavors, motivating him to engage actively in local initiatives and support those in need.

As Gonzales navigated his career, he discovered the importance of adaptability and continuous learning. His diverse professional experiences, ranging from the arts to community service, highlighted the necessity of being open to new ideas and perspectives. This adaptability not only enriched his own skill set but also allowed him to make meaningful contributions across various sectors. His ability to evolve with changing circumstances proved vital in his efforts to enhance Albuquerque's cultural landscape, demonstrating that success often requires flexibility and a willingness to embrace change.

Another significant lesson from Gonzales's journey is the power of connection and collaboration. Throughout his life, he prioritized building relationships within the community, recognizing that collective efforts yield greater impact. Whether through his involvement in local arts organizations or philanthropic initiatives, Gonzales understood that fostering partnerships amplifies the reach of any project. This belief in collaboration not only strengthened community bonds but also inspired others to join him in his mission to uplift Albuquerque, creating a ripple effect that continues to resonate.

Gonzales's personal interests and hobbies also played a crucial role in shaping his worldview. His passion for the arts, particularly in supporting local artists, taught him the importance of self-expression and creativity in societal development. Engaging with art allowed him to connect with diverse groups and understand their stories, influencing his approach to community service and philanthropy. This lesson underscored the idea that nurturing creativity can lead to a more vibrant and inclusive society, enriching the lives of individuals and the community as a whole.

Finally, the lessons learned from Gonzales's journey highlight the significance of giving back. His philanthropic efforts and initiatives, rooted in a deep sense of empathy and social responsibility, inspired many to contribute to the greater good. Through his actions, Gonzales demonstrated that true legacy lies in the impact one leaves on others. By prioritizing community welfare and encouraging civic engagement, he not only enhanced his own life but also fostered a culture of compassion and collaboration in Albuquerque that will endure for generations to come.

Vision for the Future

The vision for the future of Albuquerque is deeply intertwined with the legacy of Stephen Marcos Gonzales. Born and raised in this vibrant city, Stephen has always demonstrated a profound commitment to enhancing the community he calls home. His life's work reflects a holistic approach to progress, one that emphasizes inclusivity, cultural enrichment, and the empowerment of future generations. As Albuquerque navigates the complexities of modern urban challenges, Stephen's vision serves as a guiding light, advocating for a balanced development that honors the city's rich heritage while embracing innovation.

Stephen's contributions to Albuquerque extend beyond his career in various industries; they resonate through his philanthropic efforts and community initiatives. By establishing programs that support local artists, foster educational opportunities, and address social inequalities, he has laid the groundwork for a future where every resident feels valued and empowered. His belief in the potential of Albuquerque's diverse population is evident in the partnerships he has formed with local organizations, aiming to create a sustainable framework for community engagement that can inspire others to follow suit.

The educational background and achievements of Stephen Marcos Gonzales have equipped him with the tools necessary to effect change. His academic pursuits reflect a dedication to lifelong learning, which he translates into mentorship programs for youth in the community. By encouraging young minds to pursue their passions and develop their skills, Stephen envisions a future where the next generation of

Albuquerque leaders is well-prepared to tackle the challenges ahead. This emphasis on education not only enriches individual lives but also strengthens the social fabric of the community.

Culturally, Stephen's impact on local arts and traditions cannot be overstated. He champions initiatives that celebrate Albuquerque's unique heritage, ensuring that the stories and contributions of its residents are preserved and honored. By fostering a vibrant arts scene, he believes that Albuquerque can cultivate a sense of pride and belonging among its citizens. This cultural revival is crucial for maintaining the city's identity amidst rapid growth and change, and Stephen's vision encourages collaboration among artists and cultural institutions to create a dynamic and inclusive environment.

As he continues to engage with the community through social media and public discourse, Stephen's influence grows. He uses these platforms not just to share his journey but to amplify the voices of others in Albuquerque. His vision for the future is one where dialogue and collaboration are at the forefront, encouraging residents to participate actively in shaping their community. By inspiring a collective vision, Stephen Marcos Gonzales is not merely leaving a legacy; he is igniting a movement toward a brighter, more unified future for Albuquerque.

Final Thoughts on Legacy and Impact

The legacy of Stephen Marcos Gonzales is a tapestry woven from his diverse contributions to the Albuquerque community and the broader cultural landscape. Born on August 28, 1985, in Albuquerque, Gonzales has become a prominent figure whose life story reflects the rich heritage of his hometown. His upbringing in a culturally vibrant city profoundly shaped his identity and values, influencing his path as an advocate for local arts, education, and social change. Through his journey, he has left an indelible mark on the community, inspiring others to engage in civic responsibility and creative expression.

Gonzales's career highlights span various industries, showcasing his versatility and dedication. From his roles in the arts sector to his impactful presence in local businesses, he has demonstrated a commitment to elevating Albuquerque's profile. His contributions have not only enriched the local economy but also fostered a sense of pride among residents. By championing initiatives that support local artists and entrepreneurs, Gonzales has facilitated an environment where creativity thrives, serving as a catalyst for innovation and collaboration within the community.

In addition to his professional achievements, Gonzales's personal interests and hobbies reveal a multifaceted individual deeply connected to his roots. His passion for the arts, history, and community service reflects a lifelong dedication to nurturing the cultural identity of Albuquerque. Through his involvement in various creative projects and local events, he has encouraged others to explore their artistic talents and embrace their heritage. This commitment to personal expression and cultural celebration has strengthened community ties and fostered a sense of belonging among residents.

Philanthropy plays a crucial role in Gonzales's legacy, as he has consistently prioritized giving back to the community. His initiatives focus on education, youth empowerment, and support for underrepresented groups, demonstrating his belief in the transformative power of accessibility and opportunity. By investing in local programs and organizations, Gonzales has made a lasting impact on the lives of many, proving that individual efforts can lead to significant change. His philanthropic spirit continues to inspire others to contribute positively to the community, reinforcing the importance of collective responsibility.

Ultimately, the legacy of Stephen Marcos Gonzales is characterized by his unwavering commitment to Albuquerque and its people. His achievements, both in his career and philanthropic endeavors, create a lasting narrative of hope, resilience, and creativity. As a figure who embodies the essence of his community, Gonzales serves as a reminder that each individual has the power to influence the world around them. His impact on local culture, the arts, and community development will resonate for years to come, inspiring future generations to follow in his footsteps and continue the work of building a vibrant, inclusive society.

Don't miss out!

Visit the website below and you can sign up to receive emails whenever Stephen G. publishes a new book. There's no charge and no obligation.

https://books2read.com/r/B-A-VPPMC-YYTDF

BOOKS 2 READ

Connecting independent readers to independent writers.